Printworks
0326
D0319027

THE COOLEST JOBS ON THE PLANET

# SPECIAL EFFECTS MAKE-UP ARTIST

Jonathan Craig and Bridget Light

Raintree is an imprint of Capstone Global Library Limited, a company incorporated in England and Wales having its registered office at 7 Pilgrim Street, London, EC4V 6LB – Registered company number: 6695582

www.raintreepublishers.co.uk
myorders@raintreepublishers.co.uk

Text © Capstone Global Library Limited 2014
First published in hardback in 2014
Paperback imprint published in 2015
The moral rights of the proprietor have been asserted.

All rights reserved. No part of this publication may be reproduced in any form or by any means (including photocopying or storing it in any medium by electronic means and whether or not transiently or incidentally to some other use of this publication) without the written permission of the copyright owner, except in accordance with the provisions of the Copyright, Designs and Patents Act 1988 or under the terms of a licence issued by the Copyright Licensing Agency, Saffron House, 6–10 Kirby Street, London EC1N 8TS (www.cla.co.uk). Applications for the copyright owner's written permission should be addressed to the publisher.

Edited by Nancy Dickmann, Laura Knowles, and Helen Cox Cannons
Designed by Richard Parker and Emily Hooton at Ken Bell Graphic Design
Picture research by Mica Brancic
Production by Vicki Fitzgerald
Originated by Capstone Global Library Ltd
Printed and bound in China by CTPS

ISBN 978 1 406 25981 0 (hardback)
17 16 15 14 13
10 9 8 7 6 5 4 3 2 1

ISBN 978 1 406 25986 5 (paperback)
18 17 16 15 14
10 9 8 7 6 5 4 3 2 1

**British Library Cataloguing in Publication Data**
Craig, Jonathan.
  Special effects make-up artist. -- (The coolest jobs on the planet)
  1. Film makeup--Juvenile literature. 2. Theatrical prosthetic makeup--Juvenile literature.
  3. Makeup artists--Vocational guidance--Juvenile literature.
  I. Title II. Series III. Light, Bridget.
  792'.027-dc23

**Acknowledgements**
We would like to thank the following for permission to reproduce photographs: Alamy pp. 9 (© AF Archive), 40 (© David Taylor); Getty Images pp. 4 (Stone/Ryan McVay), 39 (Wirelmage/E. Charbonneau); Jonathan Craig pp. 5, 7, 10, 11, 13, 14, 15, 16, 17, 18 (left & right), 19, 20, 21, 22, 23, 24, 25, 26, 27, 28, 29, 30, 31, 32, 33, 34, 36 bottom, 37 top, 41; Rex Features pp. 6 (Everett Collection), 35 (Moviestore Collection), 38 (Everett Collection); Shutterstock pp. 12 (© konstantynov), 36 top (© Prezoom.nl), 37 bottom (© Thorsten Schmitt); The Kobal Collection p. 8 (Columbia).

Background design images supplied by Shutterstock (© 3d brained,© Attitude, © caesart, © ChameleonsEye, © dundanim, © Eky Studio, © foxie, © Ghenadie, © grivet, © ilolab, © isaravut, © IvicaNS, © Jacek Fulawka, © javarman, © Markus Gann, © Mika Shysh, © Miriam Doerr, © phoebe, © Skocko, © Steve Collender, © Tjeffersion, © twobee, © Vit Kovalcik).

Cover pictures of special-effects artist Steve Johnson (Ghostbusters, Species) working on model Mandi Moss reproduced with permission of Corbis (ZUMA Press/© Gene Blevins).

Every effort has been made to contact copyright holders of material reproduced in this book. Any omissions will be rectified in subsequent printings if notice is given to the publisher.

**Disclaimer**
All the internet addresses (URLs) given in this book were valid at the time of going to press. However, due to the dynamic nature of the internet, some addresses may have changed, or sites may have changed or ceased to exist since publication. While the author and publisher regret any inconvenience this may cause readers, no responsibility for any such changes can be accepted by either the author or the publisher.

LIBRARY

| CLASS NO. | 792. 027 CRA |
| ACC. NO. | 032608 |

# CONTENTS

# CINEMA MAGIC

Have you ever been scared by a creature you've seen at the cinema? Have you ever been amazed by cool make-up in a film? Have you ever wondered how they do it? I used to wonder the same thing, but now I know the answer, because that's what I do! My name is Jonathan, and I am a special effects make-up artist.

## Did you know?

The term "make-up" includes any facial and body reconstruction to create a special effect. It could be anything from green warts to a dagger in an actor's back – with lots of blood, of course!

Everybody loves being scared or amazed at the cinema.

One of my first jobs was making a real horse look like it was burnt for a film. Even though it was only a student film, it felt so rewarding to see my work on the big screen.

I have a job that is interesting, challenging, and a lot of fun! Nothing compares to transforming an ordinary looking person into something that only existed in my mind before. Looking back, I could never have imagined making a career out of doing something I love so much. Sometimes following your passion can really pay off. It's never too early to start thinking about what you love to do, and how you can make a living doing it.

## MY HERO!
## TOM SAVINI (BORN 1946)

Tom Savini did the make-up on some of my favourite horror films. He came up with brand new techniques and was a big inspiration for me getting into the business. Right after make-up school, I ended up meeting him at a convention. It was amazing.

# CHILDHOOD INSPIRATION

As a child, I loved films with puppets and amazing-looking creatures. My favourite films were made by the Jim Henson Creature Shop™. I loved everything he did, from *Sesame Street* and *The Muppet Show*, to *Labyrinth* and *Dark Crystal*.

Jim Henson

My father worked in the television industry as a set designer. His job was to find or build the main parts of a set, such as walls and windows, but also smaller details such as background items or props. I remember seeing things in the background of a television programme and realizing that my dad had borrowed them from my room. I wondered where my globe had gone!

## MY HERO!
## JIM HENSON (1936-90)

Not only was he the creator of the *Muppets* and *Sesame Street*, but he also voiced and operated many of his creations, most famously Kermit the Frog. He was the first puppeteer to create puppets with moving mouths and hands for television.

# On set

One of the productions my dad worked on was called *Under the Umbrella Tree*. It was a children's programme that featured puppets like Iggy the Iguana (left), made by Noreen Young. I got to visit my dad on the set, and the highlight of spending time there was meeting Noreen herself and hanging out with the puppeteers. The idea that you could create characters and creatures for television and films was hugely inspirational for me.

## Did you know?

The character Yoda from the *Star Wars* films *The Empire Strikes Back* (1980) and *Return of the Jedi* (1983) was voiced and puppeted by Frank Oz. Frank Oz often worked with Jim Henson. He was the original puppeteer and voice behind Miss Piggy and Fozzie Bear, among others.

# Horror films and Halloween

As I got older, I became a big fan of horror films. I was fascinated with zombies, gore, and aliens. The most fun day of the year for me was always Halloween – and it wasn't just about the free sweets! Each year, I wanted to have a scarier costume than the last.

Sometimes my uncle would buy me a make-up kit for Halloween that I could use myself. One year I got a zombie face, while another time it was a skull. Those were the first special effects (FX) make-ups I ever did.

One of my favourite films when I was young was *Close Encounters of the Third Kind*.

# Turtle power!

Probably my favourite costume as a child, was when I got to be a Ninja Turtle for Halloween. I didn't make that one myself – it was shop bought, but the original *Teenage Mutant Ninja Turtles* film (1990) was a huge inspiration for me. In the film, the costume was a suit and head that the actor wore. The heads had animatronics (when electronics are used to animate a creature) to move the facial features. It was a crazy concept, but it worked!

The costumes from the original *Teenage Mutant Ninja Turtles* really brought those characters to life.

## ESSENTIAL SKILLS

Every film or character starts with an idea. If you have an active imagination, you have the ability to come up with great ideas. Turning imagination into reality is what being a make-up artist is all about.

## Did you know?

The Jim Henson Creature Shop™ made the costumes for the original *Teenage Mutant Ninja Turtles* film and its sequel *Teenage Mutant Ninja Turtles II: The Secret of the Ooze* (1991). No wonder I loved them so much!

# A LIFE-CHANGING DECISION

Here I am shooting a film in Los Angeles, USA.

In high school, in Ottawa, Canada, I volunteered as a camera operator through a co-op programme at a local television station. They trained me and gave me the opportunity to shoot live music, sport, and local events. It eventually became a paying job and I was able to branch out and work for other stations.

I really enjoyed filming and by the time I graduated from high school, I had decided that my career would be operating a camera for television. After a few more years working in Ottawa, I moved to Toronto. In a larger city, there were more opportunities.

This is my friend Eric's Halloween costume. Even though I did the make-up myself, he creeped me out all night!

## TOOLS OF THE TRADE: PROSTHETIC TEETH

Prosthetic teeth, like these ones, can be made in the studio to fit an actor's mouth, or ordered online. Teeth are one of the things that we recognize people by. Just changing someone's teeth can make them look like an entirely different person.

# Looking for something new

My job as a camera operator was exciting – I got to travel and film interesting things. But I never stopped thinking about puppets, monsters, and make-ups. One day, I decided to look into taking a course. I didn't necessarily think this would be a new career path; I just wanted to be able to create frightening and believable Halloween make-up and masks for myself and my friends.

# Make-up school

I found that there were several certificate courses available. Certificate courses are not as broad as a university degree. They are generally shorter and more intensive, and you earn a certificate on completion.

I finally chose the School of Professional Make-Up. They offered the shortest programme (4 months), which was great for me because I didn't want to be out of work for too long. Most importantly, many of their instructors were people who had worked on my favourite horror films!

## ESSENTIAL SKILLS

Shading and colour blending are important skills because a make-up artist needs to be able to create depth and shape in a natural looking way.

Although I've never used my beauty or bridal make-up skills professionally, I could still do it, especially if it was for a zombie bride!

# Here comes the bride...?

To take the Prosthetic and Special FX make-up class, you first have to learn beauty and bridal make-up. Though I didn't really have any interest in this kind of make-up, I was willing to do whatever was required to get to the point where I could learn how to do monster and zombie make-ups.

After completing the beauty course, I realized it's important for every make-up artist to know the basics. I learned how to match skin tones, cover imperfections, and use highlighting and shadowing to emphasize certain features. All these skills are important when creating creature make-ups.

The first time I felt like a real artist was when I got my own set of make-up brushes.

## TOOLS OF THE TRADE: MAKE-UP BRUSHES

It's important to keep your brushes clean as they're expensive to replace. I have large brushes for applying powder and blusher, small thin brushes for creating veins and other fine details, and everything in between.

# Special effects and prosthetics

In the special effects part of the make-up course, I learned how to make prosthetics. A make-up prosthetic is something applied to a person that gives the illusion that it is actually part of their body. It can be as simple as a mole or as complicated as an entire creature that barely looks human.

This was my first special effects project on the course.

# Getting the design right

The first thing I was taught is that character design is very important! A special effects make-up artist needs to have information about the character they are trying to create. It could be a sketch, a photograph, or just a written description. Often, the make-up artist comes up with a sketch themselves, based on discussions with the creator. Imagination and the ability to sketch can be great assets here.

# No prosthetics required

During this part of the course, I also learned a number of out-of-kit techniques using simply make-up, paint, and wax that can be used to transform someone into a particular character. My class got to visit the set of a television programme to watch professional make-up artists in action.

## TOOLS OF THE TRADE: PORTFOLIO

A portfolio is a collection of your past work – usually photographs. Special FX make-up artists need to build a good portfolio to get work. You can start working on your portfolio at college.

## MY HEROES! MATT DEWILDE, ALLAN COOKE, AND RANDY DAUDLIN

Matt DeWilde and Allan Cooke were my prosthetic teachers at school. They are both talented sculptors and make-up artists, who not only taught me my craft, but helped me find work. Randy Daudlin was my out-of-kit teacher. I learned so much from him, too.

Matt DeWilde

I was very inspired by my teachers, including Matt DeWilde, because they were earning a living doing what I really wanted to do.

# STARTING OFF

Through the college, I was able to find some jobs. Though they were voluntary or low paying, they allowed me to build my portfolio. One of them was doing a burnt horse (see page 5) for a college film and another was a music video featuring flying monkeys. It was a spoof of *The Wizard of Oz* (1939). I had a great time doing it, and it really boosted my confidence knowing that I could pull off something that was really challenging.

## Did you know?

*The Wizard of Oz* was the first film that used foam-latex for the prosthetics. The Scarecrow, the Tin Man, the Cowardly Lion, the Wicked Witch of the West, and the Flying Monkeys all had latex features attached to them. Foam-latex is still commonly used today.

These flying monkeys are from the music video I worked on.

# Even better zombies

I was also excited to finally be able to do really professional Halloween make-up for my friends and myself. When I first started out, Halloween was a great time to practise things I'd learned in college. I made some of my friends into zombies or gave them broken noses. These were really fun to do, and I was able to use the pictures for my portfolio!

# Making a living

The film industry is a competitive business. I know many people who make a living at being make-up artists, but many of us have other jobs as well. For example, I still operate camera for television to help pay the bills. But even if I go a while without doing make-up on a production, I'm still working in my workshop. It's very important for me to keep my skills up, so I'm always trying new techniques and playing with new materials.

My latest project is sculpting a puppet based on a drawing by my sister. I hope to use this in my own production one day.

## TOOLS OF THE TRADE: SCULPTING TOOLS

Sculpting tools, such as trowels and scrapers, are used to get different textured effects on the clay. Spray bottles are used to keep water-based clay moist.

Here is a tool for cutting clay. Every job needs a different tool.

# A family affair

I come from a family of artists. After being a set designer for many years, my dad followed his passion and became a successful painter. My mother has made jewellery and owned her own animation studio. Like my dad, my sister also makes her living as a painter and my brother is a professional photographer. There are definite ups and downs working in a creative field, but it really helps to have my family – we have always supported each other in all our endeavours.

# MATERIALS

One of my favourite things to do as a make-up artist is play with gloop! There are so many different kinds of materials used in prosthetic make-up. Some of the main materials I work with are clay, concrete, alginate, silicon, gelatin, latex, foam, and foam-latex.

Here are a few of the materials that I use.

Some materials, such as clay, are used for sculpting. Others, such as concrete and alginate, are used to build moulds. The actual prosthetics that are adhered (stuck) to an actor might be made from silicon, gelatin, or foam-latex. All these materials start off as goo or powder, but they end up making something amazing!

# Safety first!

Many of the materials used in FX make-up are toxic, so it's very important when working with certain chemicals to have the right safety equipment. It's also important to make sure that any actor having a prosthetic applied is not allergic to any of the materials.

## Did you know?

Silicon is the second most abundant element in our planet's crust. Many silicone products are made using the element silicon, including cookware, contact lenses, in medical scar treatment, in sealant products for buildings, and even in shampoos and hair gels. The silicone I use comes in a two-part clear liquid, which turns to rubber when mixed together. There are hundreds of different kinds of silicone and certain jobs call for certain types. Originally, they were all created from silicon dioxide.

These are some of the things that keep me safe when I'm working with toxic chemicals. I also make sure the studio is well ventilated.

latex gloves

safety goggles

gas mask for handling toxic chemicals

Every project is different, but many can be worked on over a number of days. For this project, I was asked to create a large prosthetic nose. The nose would be used in a television programme that was conducting an experiment to see how real people would treat an actress based on the size of her nose.

Here, my friend Christina (another talented make-up artist) and I are casting the actress's face.

# Day 1: Casting a face

The actress playing the part came to my studio to have her face cast. My assistant and I cast her face using alginate (a powder mixed with water that hardens) and plaster bandage (which also hardens when wet – it is often used for casts for broken legs or arms). Once everything had hardened, I carefully removed the material.

Now I had a perfect negative of her face. That means once concrete is poured into it, I could create an exact copy of her face. I created the concrete copy to have a base for sculpting what would be the prosthetic nose. That way, it would fit over her actual face exactly.

Once the concrete has been poured into the mould, it's a case of waiting for it to harden.

negative

concrete copy

## Note to self

Always have an assistant when casting a face. They can keep an eye out to make sure that the alginate does not block someone's nasal passage,

## Did you know?

Alginate is extracted from seaweed. It doesn't taste like sushi, though! Some alginate is actually flavoured like mint for use when casting teeth. If you have braces, your dentist probably cast your teeth with alginate first.

# Day 2: Sculpting the nose

Using clay, I sculpted a new nose on top of the concrete face cast. It's always a good idea to work from photos or sketches of the prosthetic you are trying to create. For a more complicated make-up, I would spend a lot of time researching the concept, but for this project I found a photo online of a large nose and worked from that.

The clay is sculpted on to the concrete face.

## Making a mould

Once I'd sculpted the nose to my satisfaction, I was ready to move to the next step, which was creating a mould of the new nose. To make the mould, I built a wall around the face and poured in concrete. The wall is only needed until the concrete has set.

Concrete moulds take about an hour to harden, so sometimes you can start making prosthetics the same day. In this case, I left it to harden overnight. The next morning, I opened the mould and removed the clay. What was left was the concrete negative of the nose that I sculpted. I was then ready to make the actual prosthetic that the actress would wear.

Here is the two-part nose mould fitted together, with one part on top of the other.

## TOOLS OF THE TRADE: DREMEL

A Dremel can be used for cutting, sanding, and polishing different materials. For the nose mould, I used the Dremel to make three holes. When you make the second part of the mould, cement fills the three holes, and they act as keys or indicators of where the mould fits together.

## Note to self

Clay can be used for more than just sculpting. Use it to build the walls for a mould and remember to reuse old clay.

# Day 3: Making the prosthetic

For this project, I used gelatin to create the prosthetic because it sets quickly and is cheaper than some other materials. It is important to consider the budget when deciding what materials to use, and this television programme did not have a large budget.

There are downsides to using gelatin. The prosthetic can't be reused, and if it gets too hot, it will start to soften and can fall off the actor's face! This shoot was only for one day, so it was not necessary for the prosthetic to be reused.

This is the two-part mould opened up. I pour the gelatin in to the nose space.

To make the prosthetic, I heated up the gelatin in the microwave until it became a liquid, and poured it into the negative of the nose. I then pressed the second part of the mould (the concrete face cast) into it and squeezed them tightly together.

# Be patient!

Gelatin takes about 20 minutes to set and it's very important to wait until it does. If you open it too soon, you can ruin the prosthetic. Once the gelatin had set, I removed the new prosthetic nose, and it was then ready to be fitted to the actress's face.

## Note to self

Be very careful handling materials. For example, hot gelatin can burn your skin.

This is the finished nose!

## ESSENTIAL SKILL

Being able to make a mould properly is a key skill. It must be strong, clean, and most importantly, a mould that opens up! If you do not make the seam in the correct location, both sides of the mould can lock together and never open. Then you have to start from the beginning.

# Day 4: Applying the prosthetic

It was finally time to go on set and transform the actress. On the previous day, I had made five noses. I nearly always make more prosthetics than I need because if the edges are not perfect or something goes wrong with the application, I need to have back-ups, especially because gelatin prosthetics cannot be reused.

I brought the three noses that turned out the best, and using prosthetic glue I attached the best one onto the actress's real nose. I smoothed out the edges and used a solvent to dissolve them seamlessly into the skin. Once the nose was properly applied, I painted the prosthetic to match her natural skin colour.

Applying a nose to an actress on set is a tricky job.

## TOOLS OF THE TRADE: MAKE-UP REMOVER

Part of a make-up artist's job includes removing make-up when the filming is finished. Some prosthetic glue is very strong, and trying to take off a prosthetic without make-up remover could injure the actor.

## Did you know?

Nicole Kidman wore a prosthetic nose for her portrayal of Virginia Woolf in the film *The Hours* (2003). My favourite prosthetic nose, however, was a more obvious one: the nose worn by Steve Martin in the film *Roxanne* (1987).

The final product – success!

# Too hot to handle

I planned the application to take 30–45 minutes, but because the lights were so hot, the actress was sweating and the prosthetic started to become soft. The first two noses ripped, and I had to be extremely careful with the last one, but luckily everything went well.

# Day 5: Out-of kit make-up

Some prosthetic make-up is done entirely out of kit, which means that it doesn't involve a pre-made appliance or prosthetic. On set, I have to create a character or wound with whatever I have brought with me. I might use paints, make-up, and wax to create 3D wounds such as a broken nose or cut.

Wax is a great material to create different effects. It works well for wounds, because it's like adding a new layer of skin that you can then paint over – it is easy to make it appear like the skin has ripped. The effects you can get just using paint and make-up are amazing. You can make a nose look broken and swollen with highlights and shadow alone – no 3D prosthetic.

This make-up was done entirely out of kit. Paint and make-up can be used to make someone look dirty, tired, older, or more glamorous.

# Good hair day

On set, character make-up can also involve hair. I may have to apply a fake moustache or maybe a bald-cap. Before I go on set, I work out what kind of effect I will need to create and make sure I have the proper tools and materials needed.

Here are some of the items I take on set with me.

brushes

fake blood

latex

paint

wax

sponge

glue

powder

## TOOLS OF THE TRADE: AIRBRUSH

An airbrush is really useful. You spray on make-up using an air compressor, which spreads it finely enough to achieve a seamless transition of colour. It is excellent for highlights and shadows.

Doing prosthetic make-up is a complicated process, and there are plenty of opportunities for things to go wrong along the way. I have opened moulds too early, broken moulds, and mixed chemicals incorrectly, so they didn't set properly. Although I know I will continue to make mistakes, I always learn from them.

The mould broke – catastrophe!

# A problem nose

With the gelatin nose prosthetic that I worked on, I actually dropped the original nose sculpture that I'd been working on for several hours. I had to start sculpting it again from scratch! Luckily, because I started the project early, I had the time to redo it.

The edges on this make-up are too visible. Back to the drawing board!

## ESSENTIAL SKILL

You need to be clever and inventive to solve problems. On one film set, the script was changed at the last minute and they needed to make it look like a part of someone's head had been shot off. I hadn't planned for this, but I got some wax and blood from my kit and some pieces of plastic I found around the set, and was able to create something that looked very realistic.

## Note to self

Don't panic! It can make a bad situation worse. On one occasion, I was making a wound that had to bleed. The blood was held inside a latex bladder (similar to a balloon, but much thinner) underneath a skin prosthetic. This was a last-minute project and all the bladders I'd made the night before failed. I had to stay up all night remaking them. I ended up pulling it off, because I stayed calm and kept going.

33

# GAINING SKILLS

Growing up watching my favourite films, I thought make-up and prosthetics were done by people who were cleverer and more talented than I was. It wasn't until later on in life that I realized I could actually learn how to do this.

While at school, I learned some important tricks of the trade. But there are also additional classes that you can do, such as life drawing or sculpting, or classes on specific techniques like airbrushing. Make-up conventions are a great place to learn about new products and meet people in the same profession.

Here I am practising sculpting.

## Practice makes perfect!

The most important thing I've done is to continue practising what I have learned. The more you do things, the better you get. I will never stop learning or practising.

## MY HERO!
## VE NEIL (BORN 1951)

I am a long-time fan of Tim Burton films, and one of my favourites as a child was *Beetlejuice* (1988). The make-up, creatures, and effects in that film have always inspired me. The make-up artist Ve Neil won an Academy Award for her work on *Beetlejuice*. She has also won Academy Awards for *Mrs Doubtfire* (1993) and *Ed Wood* (1994). Recently, she did the make-up for *The Hunger Games* (2012).

Beetlejuice

# ESSENTIAL SKILL

To be successful, you need to be able to motivate yourself to work on your own projects and keep practising your skills, even when you're not working for someone else. It's also important to work on promoting yourself and making connections. Sometimes this business can be discouraging, as there's a lot of competition, so it's important to be able to persevere through the tough times.

# Puppets and eyeballs

To keep motivated, I spend a lot of my free time working on my own projects. One of the things I really love doing is using my FX skills to make puppets. Unlike traditional fabric puppets (like the Muppets or Fraggles), the puppets I create are usually made from silicon and are more life-like. I love creating a character and making up my own story about them. Often, I will make a short film featuring that character.

These are a number of my puppets — all personal projects.

## MY HERO!
## RICK BAKER (BORN 1950)

Rick Baker is one of the all-time great special effects make-up artists. He has won Academy Awards for seven films, including *The Nutty Professor* (1996) and *How the Grinch Stole Christmas* (2000).

Many of my masks and puppets need eyes, so I've spent a lot of time making artificial eyeballs. Making them look realistic is very difficult!

# It's alive!

Some of these puppets are operated by hand, and some by rods and cabletronics. If you plan to create a moving creature, it's good to learn about animatronics. You can give something a fairly complex range of motion, such as moving eyes or fingers, using cables and pulleys. It works in a similar way to brakes on a bicycle.

# Did anyone ask for a severed arm?

Other projects I work on in my own time are masks, body parts, teeth, and things that may end up being useful for upcoming productions. I never know when someone might call needing a severed arm for a war film!

## Did you know?

Artificial eyes were originally made out of glass. Although some are still made in this way today, it is more usual to make them out of acrylics or resins.

# HISTORY OF SPECIAL EFFECTS MAKE-UP

Using make-up for theatrical effect has been around for a long time, centuries before films were invented in the 1890s, but with the beginnings of cinema, new ideas and innovations began to change things. In the early part of the 1900s, film actors did their own make-up.

An early innovator of FX make-up was an actor called Lon Chaney. He starred in many classic films, including *The Hunchback of Notre Dame* (1923) and *Phantom of the Opera* (1925). He earned the nickname "man with a thousand faces", for his ability to transform himself using make-up.

Jack Pierce

## MY HERO!
## JACK PIERCE (1889-1968)

Jack Pierce was renowned for his out-of-kit make-up ability. He created the original Frankenstein, as well as creating the make-up for other iconic films such as *The Mummy* (1932) and *The Wolf Man* (1941).

# Using computers

In the early 1990s, CG (which stands for computer generated) became popular. Things that were once done with make-up and props were now being done with computer animation. In recent years, however, special effects make-up and practical effects (ones that are not computer generated) have made a real comeback.

Ralph Fiennes played Lord Voldemort in the *Harry Potter* films.

CG may be quicker and less expensive, but it does have limitations on how realistic it can look. These days, both CG effects and make-up effects are combined to get the best of both worlds. A good example of this is Ralph Fiennes as Lord Voldemort in the *Harry Potter* films. The make-up is real, but his nose is digitally removed.

## Did you know?

Make-up artists had to apply Harry Potter's lightning bolt-shaped scar approximately 5,800 times over the course of eight films.

39

# WHAT YOU CAN DO NOW

If you are interested in becoming a special effects make-up artist one day, or even if you just think it would be cool to do some of this stuff for fun, it's pretty easy to get started. The internet is an excellent resource for make-up tips and tricks, but the most important thing is to practise sketching and sculpting your ideas. Even if you're just using plasticine, you'd be surprised by what you can come up with. I once made a pretty realistic prosthetic finger out of play dough!

Why not try out some make-up on a friend?

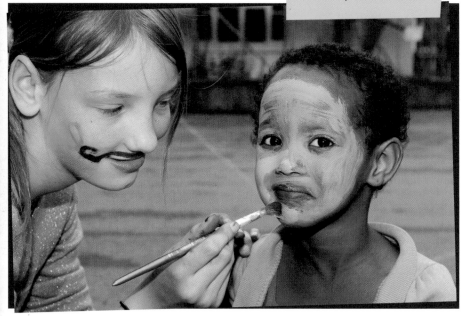

## ESSENTIAL SKILL

You need to be able to sketch, and to get across your ideas to a potential client. Someone hiring you will usually want to see what you can do before they pay you for it. This is another great reason to have a good portfolio.

# Basic equipment

There are sculpting and mould-making kits for beginners available online or at fine art and craft shops. Make-up shops and costumes shops will have starter make-up kits, or you can get some make-up and soft wax and bring your own ideas to life. There's probably even stuff around your house that you could use.

Taking art classes at school, or even outside of school to gain additional knowledge, can give you a head start. I wish I had taken more classes when I was younger.

paper

clay

pencils

brushes

## Note to self

Don't be afraid to try out your ideas – get messy, have fun, and see where your creativity can take you!

# QUIZ

See if you have what it takes to become a special effects make-up artist.

**1.  What do you most prefer to do in your spare time?**

    a) Do something active such as play football or go jogging.

    b) Draw, paint, or sculpt.

    c) Play video and computer games, or watch TV.

**2. What kind of job do you think you would like to have?**

    a) Something with a predictable schedule and income; doing the same job at the same place.

    b) Something creative and hands on; contract work with an unpredictable schedule; always doing something new.

    c) Something with a flexible schedule that you control; being your own boss.

**3. If you were working on a film, what would you like to do?**

    a) Act. I love to be the centre of attention.

    b) Make-up and effects. I'm a very visual and creative person.

    c) Direct. I like to be in charge.

    d) Write. I'm creative and like to come up with stories.

**4. If you're faced with a challenge when working on a project, how do you usually react?**

    a) Get frustrated and give up.

    b) Stay calm and try to work through the problem.

    c) Get panicky and have a meltdown.

**5. Do you think you would enjoy working on projects with lots of complicated steps that take a while to complete?**

    a) No. I get distracted easily and like to see quick results.

    b) Yes. I love a project with many steps. It feels like a real accomplishment when I'm finished.

    c) Not sure. I probably wouldn't mind if I really liked the project.

If you answered mostly Bs, it is a good indication that special effects make-up could be a great career for you!

# GLOSSARY

**acrylic** acrylic used by a special-effects make-up artist is a hard plastic used for making things like teeth prosthetics

**alginate** powder that is mixed with water to create a gooey substance that hardens in air. It is mainly used for making casts.

**animatronics** technique of making and operating lifelike robots , usually for film or television

**CG (computer generated)** use of computer graphics to create images and effects added to art, video games, or films

**convention** show or meeting. Depending on the convention, there may be people selling products, doing demonstrations, or speaking about certain topics.

**Dremel** rotary tool that has changeable heads (bits). Depending on the bit, it can be used to drill, sharpen, polish, and so on.

**foam-latex** when certain chemicals are added to latex, it can be turned into a soft light-weight foam used to make prosthetics

**gelatin** food product that is also used in FX make-up to create prosthetics

**latex** natural latex is a milky fluid that comes from plants and is used to make rubber. Latex can also be made synthetically.

**mould** block hollowed out into a shape. The mould is filled with a substance like gelatin or foam latex. When the substance hardens, the mould is opened and the substance is shaped exactly like the hollowed-out area.

**negative** in the case of a mould, the negative would be the hollowed-out area, whereas the positive would be the prosthetic created by the mould

**out-of-kit effects** effects that you create on the spot using paints, make-up, or waxes, rather than on any pre-made prosthetics

**portfolio** collection of work, usually documented by photographs, that can be easily shown to clients

**prosthetic** make-up prosthetic is something applied to a person that gives the illusion that it is actually part of their body

**resin** thick liquid that hardens into a solid substance, often transparent. Resins can be natural or synthetic.

**set designer** person whose job it is to create the look of a set. A set could be a room, a studio, a stage, or an outdoor space – any place where a production takes place.

**silicone** in FX make-up, two liquid substances are mixed to create silicone. Once hardened, it has a consistency similar to gelatin. It is used to create life-like skin texture for application as a prosthetic, or as a life-like prop.

**solvent** substance that dissolves another substance. For example, witch hazel is a solvent for gelatin.

**special effects (FX)** in TV or film, making something look real or believable without actually having to do it for real

**toxic** damaging to a living organism, such as a plant or animal. If a substance is toxic to humans, it means that it could make you ill or, if it's extremely toxic, cause death.

**visual effects supervisor** person on a production in charge of creating or managing any visual effects needed to achieve the director's vision

# FIND OUT MORE

## Books

*Film* (Behind the Scenes), Sarah Medina (Wayland, 2013)

*Film-making* (Master This), Todd Downing (Wayland, 2009)

*Film Make-up, Costumes, and Sets* (Making Films), Geoffrey M. Horn
(SOS Free Stock, 2006)

*Reel Characters*, Randy Daudlin (Two Gruesome Publishing Inc., 2010)

*So You Want to Work in Film and TV?*, Margaret McAlpine (Wayland, 2008)

*Special Make-up Effects for Stage and Screen: Making and applying prosthetics*, Todd
Debreceni (Focal Press, 2009)

## Websites

**www.dicksmithmake-up.com**

Dick Smith has worked as a make-up artist for 60 years, and has won an Academy Award for Lifetime Achievement. You can see pictures of some of his creations on his website.

**www.filmmakingforkids.com/index.html**

If you want to have a go at film-making, then have a look on this site for some interesting courses you can do.

**suite101.com/article/special-effects-makeup-for-halloween-parties-a158399**

Learn how to create some basic Halloween make-up.

# Places to visit

National Media Museum

Bradford

West Yorkshire BD1 1NQ

www.nationalmediamuseum.org.uk

Visit the cinematography section of the National Film Museum to see some amazing and rare objects connected to film history.

London Film Museum

County Hall

Queens Walk, South Bank

London SE1 7PB

www.londonfilmmuseum.com/south-bank

Learn more about film at the London Film Museum.

# Topics for further research

Why not try experimenting with make-up on your friends? Perhaps you could turn them into something scary for Halloween, or – if it's not that time of year – turn them into an animal, such as a lion? You can buy face-paint kits (including fake blood!) for a reasonable price, and it can be a good starting point in learning how to use make-up. Always make sure that you ask permission from an adult before using make-up.

# INDEX